Cursive Handwriting Workbook For Kids

Poetry & Creative Writing

A a B b C c D d E e F f G g

H h I i J j K k L l M m N n

O o P p Q q R r S s T t U u V v

W w X x Y y Z z

Motivational Practice Paper, Quotes, Poetry & Prompt Sheets
for Tracing and Mastering Cursive Letter Writing

Inside This Workbook:

Handwriting Practice

Section One

Creative Cursive Worksheets

Trace over the quote to practice then use your
cursive writing skills to complete the steps

Step 1 – Trace over the words of the motivational quote to practice

"Do what you can, with what you have, where you are."

Theodore Roosevelt

Step 2 – Now Practice writing it out yourself!

Step 3 – Write about 3 wishes that you have

Rate yourself out of 10	(Circle your score)	1 2 3 4 5 6 7 8 9 10

Step 1 – Trace over the words of the motivational quote to practice

No one is perfect – that's why pencils have erasers."
Wolfgang Riebe

Step 2 – Now Practice writing it out yourself!

Step 3 – Write about your favorite toy

Rate yourself out of 10   (Circle your score)   **1 2 3 4 5 6 7 8 9 10**

Step 1 – Trace over the words of the motivational quote to practice

You have brains in your head, you have feet in your shoes,.
You can steer yourself in any direction you choose."
Dr Suess

Step 2 – Now Practice writing it out yourself!

Step 3 – Write 3 things you really like

Rate yourself out of 10   (Circle your score)   **1 2 3 4 5 6 7 8 9 10**

Step 1 – Trace over the words of the motivational quote to practice

"It's not what happens to you, but how you react to it that matters."

By Epictetus

Step 2 – Now Practice writing it out yourself!

_____

....

_____

....

_____

....

_____

....

_____

Step 3 – Write 3 things you really dislike

_____

....

_____

....

_____

....

_____

Rate yourself out of 10	(Circle your score)	**1 2 3 4 5 6 7 8 9 10**

Step 1 – Trace over the words of the motivational quote to practice

"It's not what happens to you, but how you react to it that matters."
By Epictetus

Step 2 – Now Practice writing it out yourself!

_____

....

_____

....

_____

....

_____

....

Step 3 – Write about how you help your mom or dad (or carer)

_____

....

_____

....

_____

....

_____

| **Rate yourself out of 10** | (Circle your score) | **1 2 3 4 5 6 7 8 9 10** |

Step 1 – Trace over the words of the motivational quote to practice

"It's not what happens to you, but how you react to it that matters."

By Epictetus

Step 2 – Now Practice writing it out yourself!

_____

. . . .

_____

. . . .

_____

. . . .

_____

Step 3 – Imagine going on a trip to the moon, what did you see?

_____

. . . .

_____

. . . .

_____

. . . .

_____

| **Rate yourself out of 10** (Circle your score) | **1 2 3 4 5 6 7 8 9 10** |

Step 1 – Trace over the words of the motivational quote to practice

The more that you read, the more things you will know.
The more that you learn, the more places you'll go."
Dr Suess

Step 2 – Now Practice writing it out yourself!

Step 3 – Write about your favorite candy or snacks

Rate yourself out of 10   (Circle your score)   **1 2 3 4 5 6 7 8 9 10**

Step 1 – Trace over the words of the motivational quote to practice

"Always believe that something wonderful is about to happen"

Anonymous

Step 2 – Now Practice writing it out yourself!

Step 3 – Write 3 things that you find easy to do

Rate yourself out of 10 (Circle your score) **1 2 3 4 5 6 7 8 9 10**

Step 1 – Trace over the words of the motivational quote to practice

"I don't love studying. I hate studying.
I like learning. Learning is beautiful."
Natalie Portman

Step 2 – Now Practice writing it out yourself!

Step 3 – Write 3 things that you find hard to do

Rate yourself out of 10   (Circle your score)   **1 2 3 4 5 6 7 8 9 10**

Step 1 – Trace over the words of the motivational quote to practice

"If you have good thoughts they will shine out of your face like sunbeams and you will always look lovely."
Roald Dahl

Step 2 – Now Practice writing it out yourself!

Step 3 – Write about your best friend

Rate yourself out of 10   (Circle your score)   1 2 3 4 5 6 7 8 9 10

Step 1 – Trace over the words of the motivational quote to practice

"Never give up on what you really want to do. The person with big dreams is more powerful than one with all the facts."

Albert Einstein

Step 2 – Now Practice writing it out yourself!

Step 3 – Write about the strangest things you have ever seen

Rate yourself out of 10   (Circle your score)   **1 2 3 4 5 6 7 8 9 10**

Step 1 – Trace over the words of the motivational quote to practice

"You're braver than you believe, and stronger than you seem, and smarter than you think." – A.A. Milne I Christopher Robin

Step 2 – Now Practice writing it out yourself!

Step 3 – Write about your favorite book, why do you like it?

Rate yourself out of 10   (Circle your score)   **1 2 3 4 5 6 7 8 9 10**

Step 1 – Trace over the words of the motivational quote to practice

Why fit in when you were born to stand out?"

Dr Suess

Step 2 – Now Practice writing it out yourself!

_____

- -

_____

- -

_____

- -

_____

Step 3 – Write about your favorite song?

_____

- -

_____

- -

_____

- -

_____

Rate yourself out of 10   (Circle your score)   **1 2 3 4 5 6 7 8 9 10**

Step 1 – Trace over the words of the motivational quote to practice

Nothing is particularly hard if you break it down into small jobs".
Henry Ford

Step 2 – Now Practice writing it out yourself!

_____

_____

_____

_____

Step 3 – What would you do if you found a magic wand?

_____

_____

_____

_____

| **Rate yourself out of 10** | (Circle your score) | **1 2 3 4 5 6 7 8 9 10** |

Step 1 – Trace over the words of the motivational quote to practice

When you do the common things in life in an uncommon way, you will command the attention of the world."

George Washington Carver

Step 2 – Now Practice writing it out yourself!

Step 3 – Write something about your favorite foods

Rate yourself out of 10   (Circle your score)   1 2 3 4 5 6 7 8 9 10

Step 1 – Trace over the words of the motivational quote to practice

You cannot change the circumstances, the seasons, or the wind, but you can change yourself. That is something you have"

Jim Rohn

Step 2 – Now Practice writing it out yourself!

Step 3 – Write something about your favorite animal

Rate yourself out of 10   (Circle your score)   **1 2 3 4 5 6 7 8 9 10**

Step 1 – Trace over the words of the motivational quote to practice

"Choose your friends with caution, plan your future with purpose, and frame your life with faith."
Thomas S. Monson

Step 2 – Now Practice writing it out yourself!

_____

_____

_____

_____

_____

_____

_____

Step 3 – What makes you smile?

_____

_____

_____

_____

_____

_____

Rate yourself out of 10   (Circle your score)   **1 2 3 4 5 6 7 8 9 10**

Step 1 – Trace over the words of the motivational quote to practice

"Before you act, listen. Before you react, think. Before you spend, earn. Before you criticize, wait. Before you pray, forgive. Before you quit, try. – Ernest Hemmingway

Step 2 – Now Practice writing it out yourself!

Step 3 – What makes you sad?

| Rate yourself out of 10 | (Circle your score) | 1 2 3 4 5 6 7 8 9 10 |

Step 1 – Trace over the words of the motivational quote to practice

To accomplish great things, we must not only act, but also dream, not only plan, but also believe."

Anatole France

Step 2 – Now Practice writing it out yourself!

Step 3 – Write about your school, what do you like about it?

Rate yourself out of 10   (Circle your score)   **1 2 3 4 5 6 7 8 9 10**

Step 1 – Trace over the words of the motivational quote to practice

"Make each day your masterpiece."

John Wooden

Step 2 – Now Practice writing it out yourself!

Step 3 – Write about a holiday you had, did you enjoy it?

Rate yourself out of 10   (Circle your score)   **1 2 3 4 5 6 7 8 9 10**

Step 1 – Trace over the words of the motivational quote to practice

"All your dreams can come true if you
have the courage to pursue them."
Walt Disney

Step 2 – Now Practice writing it out yourself!

Step 3 – Write about your next birthday. What do you want to do?

Rate yourself out of 10   (Circle your score)   **1 2 3 4 5 6 7 8 9 10**

Step 1 – Trace over the words of the motivational quote to practice

"Give the world the best you have, and the best will come to you."

Madeline Bridge

Step 2 – Now Practice writing it out yourself!

_____

- -

_____

- -

_____

- -

_____

Step 3 – What do you want to be when you grow up?

_____

- -

_____

- -

_____

| **Rate yourself out of 10** | (Circle your score) | **1 2 3 4 5 6 7 8 9 10** |

Step 1 – Trace over the words of the motivational quote to practice

"Do not give up, the beginning is always the hardest."

Anonymous

Step 2 – Now Practice writing it out yourself!

Step 3 – What is your favorite thing you like to wear?

Rate yourself out of 10   (Circle your score)   **1 2 3 4 5 6 7 8 9 10**

Step 1 – Trace over the words of the motivational quote to practice

"Don't expect your friend to be a perfect person. But, help your friend to become a perfect person. That is true friendship."
Mother Teresa

Step 2 – Now Practice writing it out yourself!

Step 3 – Write something about your Teacher

Rate yourself out of 10   (Circle your score)   1 2 3 4 5 6 7 8 9 10

Step 1 – Trace over the words of the motivational quote to practice

Take every CHANCE you get in LIFE,
because some things only happens ONCE."
Anonymous

Step 2 – Now Practice writing it out yourself!

Step 3 – Write 3 things about Cats or Dogs that you know

Rate yourself out of 10   (Circle your score)   **1 2 3 4 5 6 7 8 9 10**

Step 1 – Trace over the words of the motivational quote to practice

"Winning doesn't always mean being first. Winning means you're doing better than you've done before".

Bonnie Blair

Step 2 – Now Practice writing it out yourself!

Step 3 – Write about the 3 best things about your neighborhood

Rate yourself out of 10   (Circle your score)   **1 2 3 4 5 6 7 8 9 10**

Step 1 – Trace over the words of the motivational quote to practice

"The best teachers are those who show you where to look but don't tell you what to see."

Alexandra K. Trenfor

Step 2 – Now Practice writing it out yourself!

Step 3 – When it's hot outside, I like to…….

Rate yourself out of 10   (Circle your score)   **1 2 3 4 5 6 7 8 9 10**

Step 1 – Trace over the words of the motivational quote to practice

"Don't just read the easy stuff. You may be entertained by it, but you will never grow from it."

Jim Rohn

Step 2 – Now Practice writing it out yourself!

Step 3 – When I'm happy, I like to .....

Rate yourself out of 10   (Circle your score)   **1 2 3 4 5 6 7 8 9 10**

Step 1 – Trace over the words of the motivational quote to practice

"A journey of a thousand miles begins with a single step."

Chinese Proverb

Step 2 – Now Practice writing it out yourself!

Step 3 – Write about the bravest things you have ever done

Rate yourself out of 10   (Circle your score)   **1 2 3 4 5 6 7 8 9 10**

Step 1 – Trace over the words of the motivational quote to practice

"Nothing great was ever achieved without enthusiasm".
Ralph Waldo Emerson

Step 2 – Now Practice writing it out yourself!

_____

_____

_____

_____

_____

_____

Step 3 – In 10 years time I will be ____ years old. Write about your life

_____

_____

_____

_____

Rate yourself out of 10	(Circle your score)	1 2 3 4 5 6 7 8 9 10

Step 1 – Trace over the words of the motivational quote to practice

Reach high, for stars lie hidden in your soul.
Dream deep, for every dream precedes the goal."
Ralph Vaull Starr

Step 2 – Now Practice writing it out yourself!

Step 3 – Write something about the weather today

Rate yourself out of 10   (Circle your score)   **1 2 3 4 5 6 7 8 9 10**

Step 1 – Trace over the words of the motivational quote to practice

"Only surround yourself with people who will lift you higher".

Oprah Winfrey

Step 2 – Now Practice writing it out yourself!

Step 3 – Write 3 things you could not live without

Rate yourself out of 10 (Circle your score) **1 2 3 4 5 6 7 8 9 10**

Step 1 – Trace over the words of the motivational quote to practice

The key to everything is patience. You get the chicken by hatching the egg, not by smashing it".

Arnold H. Glasow

Step 2 – Now Practice writing it out yourself!

Step 3 – Write 3 things you want to do next year

Rate yourself out of 10   (Circle your score)   **1 2 3 4 5 6 7 8 9 10**

Step 1 – Trace over the words of the motivational quote to practice

"Our attitude towards others determines their attitude towards us."

Earl Nightingale

Step 2 – Now Practice writing it out yourself!

Step 3 – The best part about my life is ......

Rate yourself out of 10	(Circle your score)	**1 2 3 4 5 6 7 8 9 10**

Step 1 – Trace over the words of the motivational quote to practice

Remember, happiness doesn't depend upon who you are or what you have; it depends solely upon what you think."

Dale Carnegie

Step 2 – Now Practice writing it out yourself!

Step 3 – Imagine you found some lost treasure, what would you do?

Rate yourself out of 10   (Circle your score)   **1 2 3 4 5 6 7 8 9 10**

Step 1 – Trace over the words of the motivational quote to practice

You don't have to be great to start but you have to start to be great."

Zig Ziglar

Step 2 – Now Practice writing it out yourself!

_____

_____

_____

_____

_____

_____

Step 3 – Where would you like to visit on a field trip?

_____

_____

_____

_____

_____

Rate yourself out of 10	(Circle your score)	**1 2 3 4 5 6 7 8 9 10**

Step 1 – Trace over the words of the motivational quote to practice

"Writing is good, thinking is better. Cleverness is good, patience is better." – Hermann Hesse

Step 2 – Now Practice writing it out yourself!

Step 3 – Write about your favorite fruit. What do you like about it?

Rate yourself out of 10   (Circle your score)   **1 2 3 4 5 6 7 8 9 10**

Step 1 – Trace over the words of the motivational quote to practice

"Whatever your hands find to do, you must do with all your heart"

John Hiatt

Step 2 – Now Practice writing it out yourself!

_____

. . . .

_____

. . . .

_____

. . . .

_____

. . . .

_____

Step 3 – Write about a vegetable that you really don't like and why

_____

. . . .

_____

. . . .

_____

. . . .

_____

| **Rate yourself out of 10** | (Circle your score) | **1 2 3 4 5 6 7 8 9 10** |

Step 1 – Trace over the words of the motivational quote to practice

Whether you think you can, or think you can't, you're right."

Henry Ford

Step 2 – Now Practice writing it out yourself!

Step 3 – Write about something special to you

Rate yourself out of 10   (Circle your score)   **1 2 3 4 5 6 7 8 9 10**

Step 1 – Trace over the words of the motivational quote to practice

"A little consideration, a little thought for others,
makes all the difference". – Eeyore

Step 2 – Now Practice writing it out yourself!

Step 3 – Write about a dream you had

Rate yourself out of 10   (Circle your score)   **1 2 3 4 5 6 7 8 9 10**

Step 1 – Trace over the words of the motivational quote to practice

"Kindness is a language that the deaf can hear and the blind can see".
Mark Twain

Step 2 – Now Practice writing it out yourself!

_____

_____

_____

_____

_____

_____

_____

Step 3 – Write about your hero

_____

_____

_____

_____

_____

Rate yourself out of 10   (Circle your score)   **1 2 3 4 5 6 7 8 9 10**

Step 1 – Trace over the words of the motivational quote to practice

"Wheresoever you go, go with all your heart."
Confucious

Step 2 – Now Practice writing it out yourself!

_____

_____

_____

_____

_____

_____

Step 3 – The 3 things I never want to do are ……

_____

_____

_____

_____

Rate yourself out of 10   (Circle your score)   **1 2 3 4 5 6 7 8 9 10**

Step 1 – Trace over the words of the motivational quote to practice

"Not only must we be good, but we must also be good for something."
Henry David Thoreau

Step 2 – Now Practice writing it out yourself!

_____

_____

_____

_____

_____

_____

Step 3 – Write a sentence about a silly monkey. What did it do?

_____

_____

_____

_____

Rate yourself out of 10   (Circle your score)   **1 2 3 4 5 6 7 8 9 10**

Step 1 – Trace over the words of the motivational quote to practice

"The time is always right to do what is right."
Martin Luther King, Jr.

Step 2 – Now Practice writing it out yourself!

_____

_____

_____

_____

_____

Step 3 – Write about your favorite movie. Why do you like it?

_____

_____

_____

_____

Rate yourself out of 10   (Circle your score)   **1 2 3 4 5 6 7 8 9 10**

Step 1 – Trace over the words of the motivational quote to practice

"Say what you mean, mean what you say, but don't say it mean".
Unknown

Step 2 – Now Practice writing it out yourself!

_____

....

_____

....

_____

....

_____

....

_____

Step 3 – Finish this sentence. There was a fat cat called ……

_____

....

_____

....

_____

....

_____

Rate yourself out of 10   (Circle your score)   **1 2 3 4 5 6 7 8 9 10**

Step 1 – Trace over the words of the motivational quote to practice

When the going gets tough try harder and you will succeed".
Unknown

Step 2 – Now Practice writing it out yourself!

_____

....

_____

....

_____

....

_____

Step 3 – Look around and list 3 things that you can see that are BLUE

_____

....

_____

....

_____

....

_____

Rate yourself out of 10   (Circle your score)   **1 2 3 4 5 6 7 8 9 10**

Step 1 – Trace over the words of the motivational quote to practice

"Do the best you can until you know better.

Then when you know better, do better." – Maya Angelou

Step 2 – Now Practice writing it out yourself!

Step 3 – Look around and list 3 things that are GREEN

Rate yourself out of 10   (Circle your score)   **1 2 3 4 5 6 7 8 9 10**

Handwriting Practice

Section Two

Creative Poetry

Trace over the poem to practice then write
the poem in the section underneath

My Cousin Has Come to Play – Ashleigh Booker

My cousin has come to play with me

I will be kind she's only three

She plays and plays no time to think

And only stops to have a drink

Butterfly - Leroy F. Jackson

Butterfly, butterfly, Sit on my chin.
Your wings are like tinsel, So yellow and thin.
Butterfly, butterfly, give me a kiss; If you give me a dozen there's nothing amiss.
Butterfly, butterfly, off to the flowers.
Wee, soulless sprite of the long summer hours.

The Bee - Edward Leary

There was an Old Man in a tree,

Who was horribly bored by a Bee;

When they said, "Does it buzz?" he replied, "Yes, it does!

It's a regular brute of a Bee

Every Piece of Candy – Lisa Bell

I'll eat every piece of candy, I'll eat every piece of cake

I'll eat all the chocolate cookies that you put upon my plate

And when there's no more left to eat I'll ask my mom for more

Because I love sweet things you see, even though I'm just four.

The Park - Ellen Witherspoon

I love going to the park

But would not go out in the dark

I'm scared of the silence in the park at night

And only go when it is bright daylight.

The Melting Snowman - Peter Matterson

We made a snowman earlier and even made a castle

But when the sun comes out to play, I know it's going to dazzle

For snowmen melt in the blazing sun, they do not stand a chance

I want to take my snowman in, so I can sing and dance

My Stomach Aches - Grace Sunderland

I ate all of your cookies then I drank all your juice

You could have told me it was sweet, my teeth nearly came loose

I'm in some pain but still can say, I'm glad I never ate the cake

Because if I did you'd laugh and say, I'm sure glad that your stomach aches

Jodi Says She's OK - Lorraine White

Jodi says she's OK, Jodi says she's fine.

Jodi stands there quietly then glances at the time

She missed the bus but there's no fuss, she'll just wait for another

Jodi says she's ok, then holds hands with her brother

My New Shoes - Kate Thomas

I got new shoes the other day, then walked right in the dirt

I should have saved them for my best and now my feelings hurt

Next time I'll wait and only wear them when I go to town

Then I'll feel great and will take my feet and walk all up and down

Spring Song - Emily Kissner

A touch of yellow, a bit of gray, a hint of green, a March day

A robin hops, a cardinal sings, a crocus blooms, hopeful things

Longer days warmer nights, wild winds, high flying kites

No more coats, geese on the wing, goodbye winter, Hello Spring!

A Day At The Zoo - Denise Jenkins

Today's the day I visit the zoo

With so many animals, I won't know what to do

I'll feed the calves and smile at the hen

and then I'll do it all again!

My Best Friends Are Here - Holly Green

My best friends are here to play

We are going to have some fun today

Messy games, playing in dirt

We'll dig until our fingers hurt!

Beautiful Flower - Scarlett Taylor

Just take a look at this lovely flower with colors so bright and fair

I might just take it home with me and put it in my hair

When not in use I'll leave it on the chair that's in my room

And when I wear it dad will say "you look like a full bloom"

Days of The Month - Unknown

Thirty days hath September, April, June, and November

February has twenty-eight alone, all the rest have thirty-one

Excepting leap year, that's the time

When February's days are twenty-nine.

Come Dance With Me – Natalie Gordon

Come dance with me, come dance with me, come dance with me I say

Let's do it now as before you know I'll have go away

Come dance with me, come dance with me, come dance with me I say

We might as well have some more fun, there's no time like today.

Combine Crew Cut - Emily Kissner

The cornfield got a crew cut, tall stalks trimmed by combine clippers

Taking some off the sides, the back, the front, leaving a stubble of stalk stumps

Except, in one forgotten spot, a place where two stalks stick up

The cornfield got a crew cut, new hairstyle for the fall.

Handwriting Practice

Section Three

Blank Handwriting Sheets

Practice your cursive handwriting with these blank handwriting sheets

Printed in Great Britain
by Amazon